INTO A LONG CURL

INTO A LONG CURL

Sakada

Black Bamboo Press
Los Angeles

Copyright © 2011 by Sakada
All rights reserved. No part of this book may be replaced or transmitted in any form or by any means, electronic or mechanical, including photocopying, recording, or by any information storage and retrieval system, without permission in writing from the publisher.

Published by Black Bamboo Press
www.blackbamboopress.com

Printed in the United States of America

Cover Design: Paul Larson
Cover Photo: Sakada
Text typeface: Hiroshige

Publisher's Cataloging in Publication
    Sakada.
        Into a long curl / Sakada.
        p. cm.
        LCCN 2011910164
        ISBN-13: 978-0615496566
        ISBN-10: 0615496563

      1. Death--Poetry. 2. Caregivers--Poetry. 3. Grief--Poetry.   I. Title.

PS3619.A399I58 2011   811'.6
                            QBI11-600120

In memory of

My father, Harry Sakada

My mother, Chiyo Sakada

and

My aunt, Nobu Isaki

GRATITUDE

This poem would not have been possible without the support, critique, and encouragement of Anne Hawthorne, Alistair McCartney, and Amanda Scott. Special thanks also to Anne Wall, Laurie Zupan, and Jennifer Calkins for reading the manuscript-in-progress. My gratitude to members of the Vesica Piscus conference; and I must acknowledge Brenda Sunoo and Jim Williams for their counsel and friendship along the way.

I also wish to thank two of my poetry mentors at Antioch: Peter Levitt, who taught me how to breathe and embrace my poetry, and Wendy Bishop, whose wonderful combination of guidance and freedom to explore allowed me to find my way into this poem. In addition, I would like to acknowledge Kate Haake, whose presence at Antioch inspired me in very special ways.

I bless Lisa Teasley for opening a door to this writing path and thank the many writers who encouraged and improved my writing in workshops along the way.

I extend a wealth of gratitude and love to those amazing people who supported me, and my parents, through the very difficult times of illness, the hardships of caregiving, and the sadness of loss. You gave in such loving and generous ways. That you didn't turn away from those difficult times is appreciated and valued. Specifically, I would like to name Dorothy Bacungan, Lillian Fritzler, and Renee Lackey. Thank you.

Additonal thanks to Paul Larson for the cover design and Kevin Knight for suggesting the perfect typeface for this poem. Also, Anna Sacks for editing.

I

An unraveling

                                                            fire.

Flames entering
with vicious intent,
red
into blood, heart, spine.
Destroying cell by cell,
devouring –

touch my hand, hold on.

Four hours
my father left on an ambulance stretcher in a hallway.
Cancer cells pushing into pain.

                                        Burning

flames torching his trembling back,
heating each breath with a moan.

Four hours
before the doctor comes.
Four hours before the order for morphine
is submitted.

                                      Darkening red.

Cancer

  in his brain
     in his lungs
         in his spine.

After brain surgery, he looked like a samurai warrior,

                        head shaved for the incision.

There was no choice,
I become caregiver. He could no longer

    complete whole sentences.

    My mother did not know what to do.
    Her own cancer would not stop.

                  Cell by cell,
            slow and vicious.

I become caregiver.

                    Pull my ear.
                    The sound of caves

                    deep in the earth.

Two surgeries, radiation, chemo.

The cold walls of the hospital,

                                        beige upon beige.

Televisions, breathing machines, floor waxers.
Filtered air sitting in each room,
collecting moments of despair,
get-well cards.

My father had visitors each day.

                                    Beige will not
                                    quench the fire.

                                    It is not satisfied.

Emergency room visits:
Fourteen times in nine months,
Seventy hours, maybe more.

"Hey baby, you looking fine."
A low, scratchy voice
vibrated over its words,
found a gap in the thin,
stained curtain that hung
between two examination rooms.
Once he caught a glimpse
of my mother, he started talking.
Others might have ignored him,
but my mother, always polite,
smiled and said "thank you."

That was all Shakey Jake needed –
a small opening. He told us
about every ailment he had:
his bursitis, the gout,
dry skin and sore throats.
Running out of symptoms
he sang songs:
Old rock and blues.
The lyrics his own.

Even my father laughed
at our night's entertainment
as we waited for another
emergency room doctor
to admit him for another
week-long hospital stay.

The next day I heard my mother
tell the nurse about the man
who told her she looked fine.

In nine months
my friend's baby
conceived, nurtured, delivered.

In the same nine months,
my father – diagnosed, cut open, medicated

dead.

His football buddies called him "Colonel."

Neighbors counted on his help.
    Waitresses saved tables for him.

The cancer was in his spine.

We brought him home to die.
He could, the doctors told us, live for two more days
or 18 months.

Three weeks — we were unable to quench the pain.

                                                          I held his hand.

Visitors all day:
He spoke with his eyes
through the burning.

I began to plan
how to let my father die,
how to help him
die.

He did not need me.
He was lost to the fire.

smoke and small bits
of memory
left on the ground.

They lifted his body
onto a stretcher.
His bones stuck
out of corners.
Their eyes carried
pity, almost shame,
imploring me
not to watch,
to hide upstairs
but I had to stay
glued, yet torn apart.
I didn't turn away
until they brought
the zipper
over his face.

Buried in echoes
I keep walking,
take myself
in search of trees
that grow up,
not down.

My father
burned to ashes.

I taste salty
breath, smell
cool rock, run my hands
along jagged walls.

I tried to remember
everything about him.
Angry at myself
for not paying more attention
to exactly who he was
when he was alive.

I built my father
into a monument,
an almost perfect
interpretation.

                        What I didn't remember
                        or didn't like,
                        I filled in.

My mother and I
argued
over anything,
everything.
She wondered
why she had been left
so human,
so fault-able.

Grass swimming:

The grass is green,
I lay my entire self
into it, moving my arms,
my legs in waves, to stir
the millions of blades
into something swirling,
something alive.

This was summer in Michigan,
my heated body loving
the cool undersides of
the lawn, swimming into
my daydreams. Holding on
to as much childhood
as I could, afraid really,
to let go of the sweetness.

And I was right, of course.
By the next summer, daydreaming
was not so simple, the lawn
burned in a dry heat.
I began my emergence
into being grown-up, the noun;
forgetting verbs and adjectives.

Leaving the lushness of grass behind.

II

Harder to measure my mother's illness
working slowly over years,
increasing its pain in hardwood notches.
When my father died, going from
healthy to dead so quickly,
my mother's disbelief and grief

gave new openings to her cancer.

                                                  Gaman –
                                                  Inner strength.

My mother was born a tiger.

                In Japan
                a woman tiger
                would bring disgrace.
                The tiger was too strong
                        for a woman.

I, a mere rooster, was always proud of her tiger-ness.

> A mother who could
> play baseball,
> hunt frogs and fossils,
> beat high school boys
> at arm wrestling.
> She carved totems
> out of telephone poles,
> created art
> out of black rocks,
> pieces of glass,
> broken tree branches.
> She built skateboards,
> playhouses,
> and terraced gardens.

            releasing fire:

The cancer worked into her bones, held on,

                        The tiger could turn on her

made itself known each day,

            in small ways, that no one else noticed

each hour. With tiger strength,

      The tiger ran out of places to go, so she went inside

for five more years she fought to live.

                I saw the scratches the tiger left,

          bits of drying blood.

Her last summer:

Friends came to say good-bye.

My mother and her sister were moving to California
to live with me.

Visitors, day after day, remembered
Mom's tootsie roll trees and painted rocks;
and the parties, so many parties,
with so much home-cooked food:
Stories about potato salad and sushi, cakes and pies.

Several people pulled me aside:
To tell me, and themselves,
that this would be the last time they would see
my mom. I just nodded.

When they left, Mom filled their arms with gifts:
everything from stained glass lamps to garden statuary;
sets of china, ceramic figurines, and flowering plants.
Then we stood on the front lawn, watching each car

until it turned the corner.

The day after Christmas she gave up the fight.

The pain, knowing it had won, lessened.
My mother began talking to those on the other side.

                                        Meeting angels.

For three weeks,
the flames lowered.

Smooth air on sharp curves.

One night, she died in the bathroom.

I lifted the dead weight of her body
back to the wheelchair, back to the bed
and after ten minutes

                                          she began to breathe again.

The next day was filled
with blue and white and glowing embers.
It was as if she was a ghost
left to say good-bye.

The afternoon light was generous, filling her bedroom.
She smiled, small upturned creases at the edges of her lips.

    careful, weightless

    I felt wings.

Her eyes, open wide and reflecting tears,
were the only things holding her head and body up.

    fragile as silk

I held her hand, the chill already beginning to take hold.
Her body translucent, soft marble,

                              holding some strange light,
                        as hummingbirds hold nectar.

There was nothing to say,
nothing more to do.

We would let her die.

I turned her hand over, and over again, amazed by its beauty.

"I have to go downstairs,"
I whispered into her right ear.

At the door, I looked back.
Her hand resting in her lap, lifted through the air,
her fingertips completed the gentlest of gestures.

Tiger strength took her on that final leap

                                        into silent air,
                                        into clouds –

      she became sky.

                                        Gaman.

                              a dark pool –
                              no reflected light.

My mother, my mirror –
the woman who loved me

gone.

I can no longer put my hand on her shoulder,
argue with her, laugh with her.

I can no longer ask her how to make her recipes,
watch her cut cookies, hear her voice.

                              I am
                              without her.

Fire burns into hidden places:

Burned tree trunks twist towards earth.
Blackened bark cracks open.
Stammering smells of dust and ash.

                        A landscape of fire's ambition
                        to place its mark
                        on green and brown.

I search this place – wanting fire to answer me,
to admit its sins, ask forgiveness
for taking my mother and my father.

        The fire only tips its rage at me,
        refuses to be apologetic.
        It lives as it knows how –
        inhaling the air it takes from others.
        Leaves soot stains, smug and engrained.

III

Mom flew away.

                    Leaving Nana, her sister, with me.

A slight leaf floating in the wind,
mixing her white light with the colors of pansies.
Nana blossomed upward, but stayed two more years.

In the last four months her breath shortened,

                her air turned to smoke,
                she needed constant care.

Nana found home with me:

She took up meditation and Tai Chi,
tended the garden, bringing in cut flowers for our tables,
startled the dinner guests with racy jokes.

Beautiful at 85.

                                        I could not think
                                        about what was happening,

                                        I could not think
                                        about saying good-bye

                                        again.

Hers was a quiet fire:

        Nothing to do but wait, wait
        for the doctor to come by
        for a minute, to tell us
        that he didn't have those test results,
        to say he was busy, would come by later.

I would sit in a hard chair by the window.
Nana, no bigger than a child,
lost in the middle of her large hospital bed.

We knew all the nurses,
had given them flowers
and cookies on other visits,

but still, they had little time.

So I cleaned up for Nana,
cut her meat,
got her fresh water.

                                          And we waited.

Knowing
it was not the doctors we were waiting for;
knowing the answers were with the angels

White feathers brushed through me.

We waited five days

before the doctors sent Nana home.
In four days we were back again.

STAT

was supposed to be written
on the blood order. Meaning
that it was important,
of highest priority.
But the nurse forgot
so we waited all day
for the last blood transfusion
to give Nana the strength
to leave the hospital.

She wanted to see her flowers
so she survived the day.
It was midnight by the time
the ambulance drove her home.
As they pulled the stretcher down,
she cried out, surprising us all, pointing
to the starry night, so happy
for such a treat.

Her last night: Nana tried to walk.
Her joints, crowded with arthritis, locked into knots.
Her legs, the strength of straw, could not hold her up.

I finally set her down in a chair next to the bed.

She asked for rice and tea.
I took this as a sign she would gain her strength,
walk across the room, be well again.

But in the morning

       My own body hardly able to move,
       exhaustion in every crevice.

       I sat beside her bed giving her drops of morphine,
       no longer worrying about overdoses or side effects.

                                 Smothering flames.

First I talked. Telling her not to be afraid. Telling her anything I could think of. Telling her I loved her.

She waved her hand to stop me.

　　　　　Fire burning slowly,
　　　　　red and white blood cells
　　　　　consumed.

Her skin spread thinly over bones.
Her body bled at the slightest touch.
Her lungs were filled with heavy fluid.
Weakness gathered in each cell.

Seventy three pounds, and pain.

　　　　　　　We listened to Elvis: Amazing Grace.

Leaving:

I could not stop
the coolness
moving up her body.
Her feet and legs
already gone.

I lay beside her,
wanting my body's warmth
to move into her. I held
my hand carefully
over her chest
as her breath continued
to soften,
her cotton nightgown
barely rising.

Air blew into us,
lifting her, leaving me
alone on the bed.
Now even her face
cooled to stillness.

I asked God to heal her, or take her.
He took her.

Later that afternoon,
after the funeral home
had taken Nana's body,
after friends, running out
of things to say, had left,
I lay down on her bed.

I woke to a view of the sky,
wind arranging the clouds
into spaces blue and clear.
Within minutes I fell back
asleep until morning.

IV

I twist my arm free.
Stars drop their light.
My bare feet sink.
Waves rise.

I stretch my body into a long curl and collapse.

Tired.

Not just my muscles, even my bones
and organs strained to move.

Defeat and relief mixed together
and surrounded the inside of my body.

Months of watching them evaporate
into more and more pain.

Hearing their last breaths,
feeling the coldness
of their empty bodies,

                                        closing their eyes.

The air would stand still for weeks,
not knowing which way to blow.

I closed myself into fetal positions,
unable to lift the layer of dead leaves.

Drowning:

After the first weeks,
you notice the hole
that has opened in your heart,
letting in a flood, the seawater
submerges and holds you.

        Drifting down
        into weaving seagrass.
        I could easily
        tangle my legs,
        become anchored
        to the ocean floor.

        Still, I cannot resist
        this need to fall,
        to grieve the things
        that have changed at the surface.
        I will breathe air again,

                but not now.

Your body, suspended:
Limbs float
as if they are doing
something useful.

The embrace of water
after so much fire.

Later, the water will pick up current.

after life:

I am left with a strange weight that ties me to their deaths.

A wounded deer:
I aim at myself, point blank,
wondering what I could have done to keep them alive.

I sat helpless beside them, watched them die.

Allow the water to carry you.
Choose not to drown.

One day, lifted by winged light
you will be delivered
to the surface.

You will remember air.

V

Come back in.
Blue streaks
beyond my vision.
White spaces.

Hold me in the light
as I twirl away
to a place that rises

                              above me.

There is suddenly a space

where your mother,
a friend, a lover,
your husband
once lived.
The space suspends
itself around you,
nudges you at night,
folds into your day.

At first, you want to honor
the space, not fill it
with anything. You find
yourself looking deeply
into it – as if for answers.
You lie down in the space,
touch its edges, willowed softness
brushes your skin.
You fall away.

One day the space calls to you.
Asks for a cracked opening to sky,
a green flowering plant,
and a favorite book.
Then a few photographs,
a worn shirt, a full meal.
Before you know it,
you are decorating, filling,
designing new uses
for this space –
glistening into it,
lifting around it.

And the person who left you the space
can rise even higher

knowing you are not so sad.

Years later,
I am just beginning to take whole breaths –

Messages: Pull my ear

"When God calls me and I go,
 I'm going to tell him how wonderful you are"

                    never worried about the weight I carried,

The sound of caves:

My father sends dolphins,
my mother butterflies.
Nana sends orchid blossoms

Some friends nod quietly at my stories,
are glad that I am finding solace in nature.
Other friends just ask me how my parents are doing,
                    and I say fine, just fine.

                    thankful for learning to carry it,

for knowing that once picked up,
a weight can lighten as easily as light dances
through tree limbs.

When I was young
I collected butterflies,
making them dead
trophies in a glassed-in box
where their wings crumbled
into gray dust. I had been told
that honoring meant possessing,
keeping forever.

I did not yet understand
the undersides of leaves
or the backs of flowers.
I had never held on to something
with the strength of my fingertips,
as a starfish holds to its rock home,
against tides moving in and out.
I had not yet held the body
of someone as they died.

Long roads
stretch out before me.
Yellow poppies
drop their petals
into black soil.
I marvel at the butterfly's wings,
pray that I too can be beautiful.

I wave my hand
to feel the wind.
Gravity defies me.
I drop down a cliff,
scraping my fingers
on sheer rock edges.
Falling into my life.
I can land on my back
or flip over,
do a swan dive
into curling ocean waves.

My body floats
into the gentle grass
of a mountain summer,
remembering what keeps the sun
coming back to the sky each morning.
Simmering heat puts me to sleep.

Lovers and strangers
shape my landscape.
I plant my feet on brittle desert ground.
Add water, sink my toes into mud.

AFTERWORD

While I believe the poem is more "important" than how I got here, how I got here "is" the poem. In this case, the experience I write of and the writing of it both started with a sense of the broken, both required and gave a breaking open, and both opened into things I never imagined possible.

I had been writing, or I should say writing around, this poem for years. Yet it was not saying what I wanted to say – or more accurately, it was not saying what I felt but had not yet been able to say. I realized I needed to go deeper.

This realization came in what you might want to call a lightning bolt, or a slight breeze, or both at once. It came suddenly over years. I was finally willing to begin again, willing to start at page zero – which is what you do when you lose a loved one, and willing to risk the opening, even if it might feel like a tear, an injury, a wound – which is what caregiving feels like.

I realized that I had to allow myself to be opened – both in terms of my perception of the experience and in terms of my writing. This required a breaking open because one cannot go deeper against a solid wall. And I had to go so far inside that I ended up outside – turning inside out. As accepting the role of caregiver required me to expand myself, sometimes beyond comfort, so does poetry.

This realization did not come alone. Such work requires courage and courage was possible for me because I had people supporting me in it – again mirroring life. I could not have done the caregiving or gotten through the grief without the support of many. This new beginning with the poem began for me after a night of workshopping with writers I respect and love; this new beginning was possible because of them. We do not really write alone.

I needed to let go. A blank page... and a word came. I resisted it, rejected it, but it was persistent and I finally wrote it down: "unraveling." And the mere act of writing the word became the force that unraveled me, and the poem. Words flowed – I didn't think, I didn't judge. I couldn't work fast enough as words spilled into place.

The poem finally had a breath of its own, its own legs to stand on, and its own heartbeat. Words settled onto the page, allowing space to fill in around them. The page itself became a canvas. I gave up my control of the story and it fell into place. I came to terms with the idea of fragments and how they can make a whole, again mirroring life, especially life during a crisis or illness.

The irony was that this poem about death had finally come to life, to its own energy. I understand how the words came spilling out, out of the broken place and into an opening. I know that breaking came in the first place because I was willing to love something – my parents and writing, and therefore willing to risk myself for this love. I am grateful – for the breaking open, and the love.

Sakada
www.intoalongcurl.com

www.ingramcontent.com/pod-product-compliance
Lightning Source LLC
LaVergne TN
LVHW051151080426
835508LV00021B/2584